# THE AWESOME BOOK OF

**WORLD OF WONDER**
**WOW**

# MONSTERS OF THE DEEP

Get ready to hear your kids say, "Wow! That's awesome!" as they dive into this fun, informative, question-answering series of books! Students—and teachers and parents—will learn things about the world around them that they never knew before!

This approach to education seeks to promote an interest in learning by answering questions kids have always wondered about. When books answer questions that kids already want to know the answers to, kids love to read those books, fostering a love for reading and learning, the true keys to lifelong education.

Colorful graphics are labeled and explained to connect with visual learners, while in-depth explanations of each subject will connect with those who prefer reading or listening as their learning style.

This educational series makes learning fun through many levels of interaction. The in-depth information combined with fantastic illustrations promote learning and retention, while question and answer boxes reinforce the subject matter to promote higher order thinking.

Teachers and parents love this series because it engages young people, sparking an interest and desire in learning. It doesn't feel like work to learn about a new subject with books this interactive and interesting.

This set of books will be an addition to your home or classroom library that everyone will enjoy. And, before you know it, you, too, will be saying, "Wow! That's awesome!"

*"People cannot learn by having information pressed into their brains. Knowledge has to be sucked into the brain, not pushed in. First, one must create a state of mind that craves knowledge, interest, and wonder. You can teach only by creating an urge to know." - Victor Weisskopf*

© 2012 Flowerpot Press

Contents under license from Aladdin Books Ltd.

Flowerpot Press
142 2nd Avenue North
Franklin, TN 37064

Flowerpot Press is a division of Kamalu, LLC, Franklin, TN, U.S.A., and Mitso Media, Inc., Oakville, ON, Canada.

ISBN 978-1-77093-810-6

Illustrators:
John Marius Butler
Robin Carter
Roy Coombs
Piers Harper
Darren Harvey
Francis Phillipps
Jonathan Pointer
Steve Roberts
Richard Rockwood
Stephen Sweet
Ian Thompson
Ross Watton (SGA)
Cartoons: Jo Moore

American Edition Editor:
Johannah Gilman Paiva

Designer: Flick, Book Design & Graphics Simon Morse

American Redesign:
Jonas Fearon Bell

Printed in China.

# CONTENTS

# INTRODUCTION

Some ocean giants, such as baleen whales, are monstrous in size, but are gentle creatures. Others, however, are killers. Man-eating sharks and poisonous jellyfish that can kill a person in under a minute roam the world's seas. Some of the fiercest deep-sea monsters are tiny. They glow in the dark, lure victims to their death, and have scary teeth—nature's way of equipping them for survival in the alien world of the deep sea. And there may be far more monsters in the ocean than we think—many sightings of odd creatures remain a mystery.

Spot and count!

**Q:** Why watch out for these boxes?

**A:** They give answers to the monster questions you always wanted to ask.

Zoom in on...

## Bits and Pieces

Look out for these boxes to take a closer look at the features of certain animals or places.

### Awesome Facts
Watch out for these diamonds to learn more about the truly weird and wonderful facts about amazing creatures of the deep-sea and their murky world.

# OCEAN LAYERS

The ocean can be divided into layers according to the depth of the water and the amount of sunlight received. The real giants, such as whales, live in the upper layers, while the more bizarre monsters—at least to our eyes—live in the depths.

The surface zone is the layer near the surface of the open ocean. Here, the sun warms the water, and sunlight enables phytoplankton (tiny plant organisms) to grow. This is the basic food on which most animals in the sea depend.

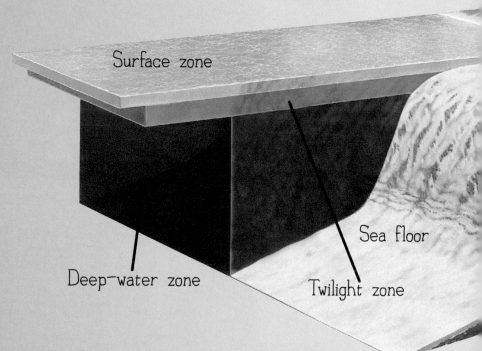

Surface zone

Sea floor

Deep-water zone

Twilight zone

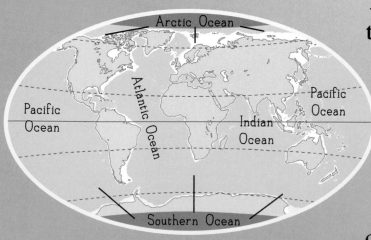

Arctic Ocean

Atlantic Ocean

Pacific Ocean

Pacific Ocean

Indian Ocean

Southern Ocean

The world's oceans cover nearly three-quarters of the Earth's surface: of the 200 million square miles (510 million square kilometers) of Earth's surface, about 140 million square miles (360 million square kilometers) are oceans and seas. Nearly all this water is over 650 feet (200 meters) deep.

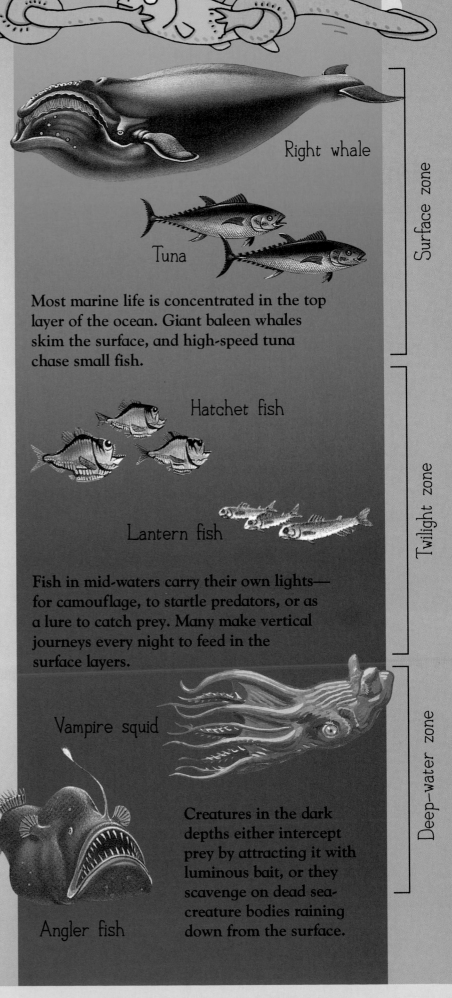

The twilight zone is the mid-water layer between 650 and 3,280 feet (200 and 1,000 meters) deep, reached by little sunlight. Many animals here are red; because water absorbs the color red, the creatures are nearly invisible.

Right whale

Tuna

Most marine life is concentrated in the top layer of the ocean. Giant baleen whales skim the surface, and high-speed tuna chase small fish.

Hatchet fish

Lantern fish

Fish in mid-waters carry their own lights—for camouflage, to startle predators, or as a lure to catch prey. Many make vertical journeys every night to feed in the surface layers.

The deep-water zone is where almost no sunlight penetrates. There are no plants in these murky depths, so deep-sea creatures have to eat what they can get. The slithery hagfish (above) feeds on the tissues of dead animals.

Vampire squid

Angler fish

Creatures in the dark depths either intercept prey by attracting it with luminous bait, or they scavenge on dead sea-creature bodies raining down from the surface.

Surface zone

Twilight zone

Deep-water zone

# DISCOVERING NEW WORLDS

Most of the oceans are unexplored. It has been said that there are more footsteps on the moon than on the bottom of the deep sea. The oceans are so vast that even big marine creatures have been able to avoid being seen by people. Many of the "new" sea animals are now being discovered.

At the bottom of the deep sea is a recently discovered world that centers not on sunlight, but on underwater hot springs heated by the Earth's molten core. Sulfur in the water feeds bacteria that, in turn, fuel a whole community of odd animals, such as 6.5-foot (2-meter) long red worms and giant clams.

## Zoom in on...

### Big mouth

In 1976, a megamouth shark 18 feet (5.5 meters) long was caught in the Pacific Ocean. Until that day, nobody knew it even existed, and only a few have been found since. It feeds on deep-sea shrimp by filtering them from mid-water areas.

The tripod fish lives on the bottom of the deep sea. It has long, feeler-like pectoral fins that it appears to use as landing gear. It springs slowly across the seabed like a grasshopper.

**Awesome Facts**

While there are 20 million light-sensitive rods in the whole of the human eye, the rattail's eye has 20 million of them in an area the size of this "o."

The rattail, or grenadier, is the most common of all deep-sea bottom-dwelling fish. It varies in length from 8 to 40 inches (20 to 100 centimeters), and it grunts using its swim bladder. Its large eyes are extremely sensitive.

# THE BIG BLUE

Baleen whales range in size from the colossal 108-foot (33-meter) long blue whale to the 20-foot (6-meter) long pygmy right whale. Slow-swimming right and bowhead whales skim the surface, gray whales often feed on the seabed, and fast-swimming fin whales take gulps of krill, fish, and seawater.

The blue whale is the world's largest living animal. It also has the world's loudest voice—a 30-second-long low-frequency moan that can be heard hundreds of miles across the ocean. The blue whale is found in all of the oceans and migrates between breeding sites in tropical seas and feeding grounds nearer the poles.

## Awesome Facts

The blue whale almost became extinct because of whaling, but a ban has meant populations are recovering. There are now between 5,000 and 10,000 blue whales worldwide.

## Filter Feeding

The right whale is recognized by the white crusty "callosities" on its head. Like all baleen whales, it is a filter feeder. It skims surface waters, filtering out krill and copepods (tiny shellfish) with long, comb-like baleen plates in its upper jaw. The plates are modified teeth. If prey is densely concentrated, several whales will feed side-by-side.

# KILLERS!

Sharks are the most feared animals in the sea. They have excellent hearing and can even detect the electronic field surrounding other creatures. Although attacks are rare, several kinds of shark will eat people. The tiger shark, up to 18 feet (5.5 meters) long, eats just about anything—including rubber tires!

**Q: Why do some sharks prod their prey?**

**A:** The oceanic whitetip shark will eat what it can get. It scours the open ocean for food and always turns up at mid-ocean disasters. Unlike other sharks, which circle a victim before attacking, the oceanic whitetip rushes in, bumps its target to assess its food value, and then takes a bite!

**Awesome Facts**

The bull shark is thought to be one of the world's most dangerous sharks. It attacks in rivers and lakes, where it goes to give birth.

The great white shark is a monster man-eater—the largest predatory fish in the sea, and the number one people killer. It grows up to 22 feet (6.6 meters) long. It prefers to eat seals, but swimmers or surfers near seal breeding colonies are at risk of being attacked, mostly as a case of mistaken identity.

How many
teeth can
you count?

When sharks get very excited by a sudden glut of food, their sensory systems become overloaded and they indulge in a wild feeding session, known as a "feeding frenzy." Sharks generally tend to avoid each other, but larger sharks may show their strength by slashing at smaller sharks during a frenzy.

# DEADLY JELLIES

Jellyfish are made of 95 percent water. They may appear to be simple creatures, but they pack a deadly punch. Their tentacles are long lines with stinging cells that can inject venom with tiny harpoons. The release of a harpoon is one of the fastest actions in nature, taking just 3 milliseconds from the moment of being touched.

Zoom in on...

## Poison Stinger

The box jellyfish, or sea wasp, is the ocean's deadliest jellyfish, and one of the most venomous animals on the planet. Its 10-foot (3-meter) long tentacles have stinging cells containing nerve poisons that can stop a human heart in 30 seconds. It has sensors that "see," and it uses jet propulsion to swim, so it is not dependent on the wind or currents.

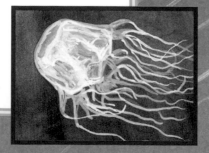

## Awesome Facts

When a Portuguese man-of-war's tentacles trap food, they contract from 30 feet (10 meters) to 4 inches (10 centimeters) in seconds, drawing the food up to the polyps.

The world's biggest jellyfish is the Arctic lion's mane jellyfish, with a bell up to 7 feet (2 meters) across and tentacles that trail 115 feet (35 meters) in the water. It catches any creature that brushes against its battery of stinging cells—except the young fish called "whiting," which hide in the tentacles and seem to be immune to the stings.

**Q: When is a jellyfish not a jellyfish?**

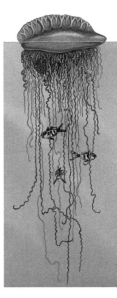

**A:** When it's a Portuguese man-of-war. This is not a true jellyfish, but a close relative called a "siphonophore." It has a balloon-like float and up to 30 feet (10 meters) of stinging tentacles trailing below. It is actually a colony of polyps, each with a different task—some deal with feeding, while other focus on reproduction.

# GIANT FISH

Some of the largest fish in the sea are also the gentlest. The whale shark is the biggest and it is a filter feeder, eating only plankton, krill, and small fish. It turns up in great numbers at coral reefs, not long after all the corals have spawned and its prey is well-fed on coral spawn.

The whale shark grows up to 50 feet (15 meters) long. It has a wide, slit-like mouth and spotted skin. Its skin and underlying muscle are tough, like a tractor tire, so they are difficult to penetrate with spears, harpoons, or even bullets. Why it has such a bright pattern on its skin remains a mystery.

The world's largest bony fish is the ocean sunfish. This enormous disk-shaped fish can be 10 feet (3 meters) long, measure 13 feet (4 meters) between top and bottom fins, and weigh up to 5,000 pounds (2,250 kilograms). It has a tiny mouth for its size, and eats jellyfish and other soft-bodied marine creatures.

Zoom in on...

## Manta Rays

The manta ray is the world's largest ray. It has a "wingspan" of up to 30 feet (9 meters), and a distinctive cephalic lobe (horn) on either side of its head. The ray is another filter feeder, harmless to people, and uses its horns to guide plankton into its broad mouth. When the feeding is good, many rays follow each other, head to tail, through the plankton swarm.

# STUPENDOUS SQUID

There are several species of giant squid, but the biggest of all is Architeuthis. It has enormous eyes, eight arms, and two long tentacles with suckered pads on the end. It is thought that within months, it can grow from a tiny baby to 56 feet (17 meters) long.

## Talking Squid

Squid communicate by changing the color and pattern of their skin. For example, when squid mate, the males turn bright red. Some researchers believe that squid have a language that rivals that of humans—a subtle skin language of ever-changing patterns.

Zoom in on...

The Humboldt Current squid that lives off the Pacific coast of South and Central America is extremely dangerous to people. It is about 10 feet (3 meters) long and hunts at night. Several underwater cameramen have been attacked and nearly drowned by a pack of these squid.

Giant squid were once thought to be a myth, but the first one was found off Denmark in 1853. Then, in 1873, some Newfoundland fishermen were attacked by a giant squid they found flailing about on the surface. It was then realized that the giant squid was not only real, but could also be dangerous to humans.

# ENORMOUS INVERTEBRATES

There are many giant invertebrates (animals with no backbones) under the sea. These include squid, crabs, huge clams in the Indian and Pacific Oceans, starfish over 3 feet (1 meter) across in the North Pacific, and oversized sea anemones off Australia.

### Awesome Facts

The world's most dangerous octopus is the blue-ringed octopus of Australia. With a single poisonous bite, it delivers enough venom to kill seven people.

The Japanese spider crab is the largest known crustacean (shelled creature). It is confined to the deep waters off the southeast coast of Japan. The largest known was a male with a leg span of 12 feet (3.7 meters), but even bigger crabs may exist.

The Pacific giant octopus is the world's largest, with tentacles spreading up to 23 feet (7 meters). It lives in the Pacific Northwest. If a giant octopus has a firm grasp on the rocky bottom, it can grab a human victim and drown him.

**?** Q: What was the biggest lobster ever caught?

A: A North Atlantic or American lobster caught off Nova Scotia, Canada, in February 1977 was over 3 feet (1 meter) long and weighed over 44 pounds (20 kilograms). It was displayed live in a New York restaurant for many years.

# DINGY DEPTHS

The Earth's surface is covered with constantly moving crustal plates that float on its molten (hot liquid) core. Where plates collide, one is sometimes pushed under the other. This is called a "subduction zone." Here, the seabed is pulled down to form deep-sea trenches, the deepest places in the ocean. Animals that survive here are mainly invertebrates, like worms.

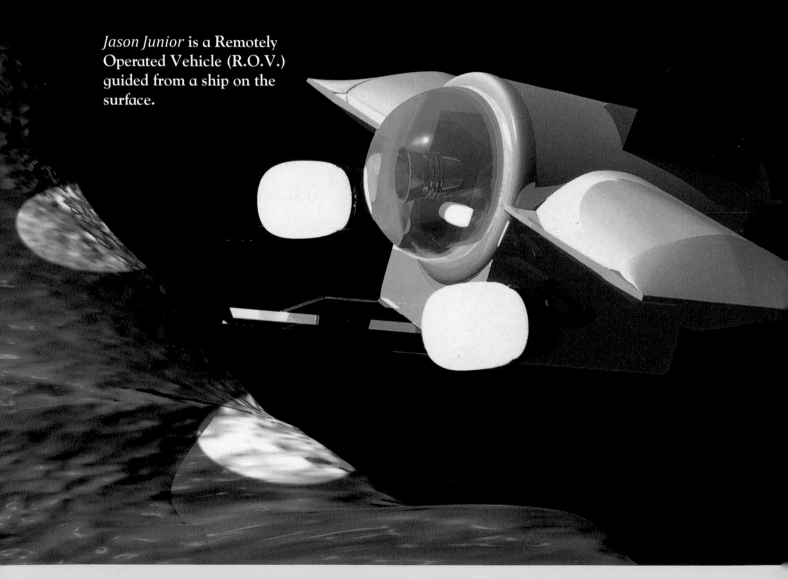

*Jason Junior* is a Remotely Operated Vehicle (R.O.V.) guided from a ship on the surface.

Only very specialized manned submersibles, which are specially reinforced to withstand tremendous pressure, can venture into deep-sea trenches. The U.S. Navy's *Trieste* was such a vessel, and it was taken to the bottom of the Challenger Deep in 1960.

Scientists can explore deep-sea areas using manned submersibles or vessels like *Jason Junior*, which they guide from surface ships. They watch a video screen and steer the vessel with a joystick. A bank of bright lights illuminates the dark ocean ahead.

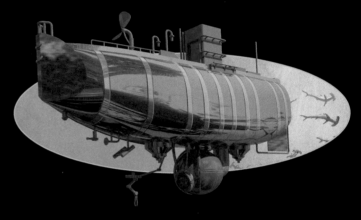

Zoom in on...

## Marianas Trench

The Marianas Trench is the deepest place on the planet. Located east of the Mariana Islands in the western Pacific Ocean, it is 1,400 miles (2,250 kilometers) long and 45 miles (70 kilometers) wide. The Challenger Deep, its deepest part, is nearly 7 miles (11 kilometers) below the surface.

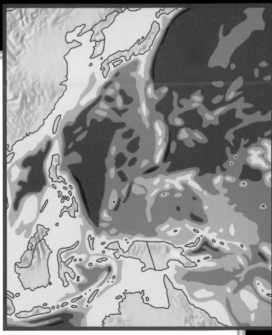

# MURKY MONSTERS

Most deep-sea "monsters" look fearsome, but many are no more than a few inches long. They have very large eyes, which help them to see in the faint light that reaches the depths. Some have eyes that look directly upward, so they can spot prey silhouetted against the dim surface glow.

The 5-foot (1.5 meter) long gulper eel is all mouth, stomach, and slender tail, and little else. Its eyes are only 1 inch (2.5 centimeters) across, and it has only a tiny brain. It lives as deep as 10,000 feet (3,000 meters).

The viperfish is only about a foot (30 centimeters) long, but it is the deep sea's most terrible predator. It has huge teeth and luminous patches in its mouth that attract prey. Some species have long "whiskers," or barbels, which hang down from under their jaws.

One of the strangest deep-sea fish must be the recently discovered winteria. It has a pair of enormous tubular eyes that concentrate the light from one direction only. It has very acute vision. Scientists discover a new deep-sea species like this about every 10 days.

# UNDERWATER MOUNTAINS

The ocean floor not only has deep trenches, it also has mountains, just as on land. Some of these seamounts are volcanoes that reach the surface to form islands and atolls. They attract wildlife, both above and below the surface. Seabirds nest on top, while enormous shoals of fish swirl around below.

How many marlin can you count?

Goatfish

Jack

### Awesome Facts
In 1963, an underwater volcano on the Mid-Atlantic Ridge exploded into the air to the south of Iceland, creating a new island called Surtsey.

Hammerhead
shark

A seamount is like an underwater oasis in the vast open ocean, and it is also a refuge. Hammerhead sharks swim aimlessly around in huge schools. In the evening, the schools break up and the sharks go hunting in small groups. The agile marlin is a hunting machine—it catches prey, such as tuna, and even squid, by slashing it with its sword-like snout.

Tuna

Marlin

Zoom in on...

## Mid-Atlantic Ridge

Snaking its way around the world at the bottom of the sea is the mid-oceanic ridge system, a chain of mountains that runs 45,000 miles (72,500 kilometers) and includes the Mid-Atlantic Ridge. The ridge forms where magma oozes up between the Earth's crustal plates. It is the most volcanically active area on the planet, and has been called "the wound that never heals."

Seamount

Mid-Atlantic
Ridge

Plates pull
apart

Trench

Magma rises

# MYSTERY MONSTERS

Ever since people have been going to sea, they have spotted unidentified monsters. Often people find curiously shaped creatures not resembling any known animal. Many are snake-like or dragon-like. Are they imaginary—perhaps the result of too many days at sea? Or could they be giant sea creatures that scientists have yet to identify?

In 1830, *H.S.S. Fly* was on duty in the Gulf of California when the crew spotted a "large marine animal with the head and general figure of an alligator," except that rather than legs, its limbs were two pairs of flippers, like those of a sea turtle. It was chasing fish. Its identity remains a mystery today.

In 1985, two brothers saw a mystery monster from their car parked by San Francisco Harbor. It was an extraordinary snake-like animal, but flexed its long body vertically rather than horizontally, like a snake. It seemed to be chasing seals.

How many sailors can you count?

# MONSTERS EXPOSED

Many sea monster sightings turn out to be perfectly ordinary things. From a distance, floating tree trunks can resemble long-necked monsters, and a riptide can look like the wake of a large animal under the surface. A line of dolphins or seals can seem like a humped sea serpent, as can a flight of low-flying cormorants or ducks.

 **Q: What's a commonly mistaken "sea monster?"**

**A:** The world's largest turtle, the leatherback, is 7 feet (2 meters) long and swims great distances. If it suddenly pops up beside a fishing boat, it could well be mistaken for a prehistoric monster.

The oarfish, or king of the herrings, might be mistaken for a sea monster. This strange ribbon-like fish, which can be up to 50 feet (15 meters) long, can look like a sea serpent at the surface of the water. It is silvery colored and has a crest of long red spines on its head that can be erected into a crown-like plume.

A rare sea mammal called the "dugong," which lives mainly in coastal waters in southern Asia and northern Australia, is the most likely explanation for the legendary mermaid. The female dugong has obvious breasts and sometime holds her young in her arms when suckling. The dugong is related to the manatee, which lives along North American shores.

## Awesome Facts

When a basking shark dies and decomposes, its gill area falls away first, leaving a shape that looks like a long-necked prehistoric creature called a "plesiosaur."

# ENDANGERED RECORD BREAKERS

Some of the largest animals ever to have lived are found in the sea today, but many of them are endangered. These record breakers have been the most desirable animals to catch, and they are also among the most vulnerable. The largest are often breeding females—when they are gone, the species becomes extinct.

Just how big are monsters of the deep? The picture below shows the average relative size of some of the oceans' largest animals compared to a human. The very biggest, the blue whale, is an endangered species.

## Record-Breaking Monsters

**Blue whale:** 112 feet (34 meters) long; Southern Ocean

**Sperm whale:** 68 feet (20.7 meters) long; Pacific Ocean

**Giant squid:** 56 feet (17 meters) long; beached in Newfoundland

**Whale shark:** 42 feet (12.65 meters) long; off Pakistan

**Manta ray:** can have a wingspan of 30 feet (9 meters)

**Great white shark:** rarely exceeds 23 feet (7 meters)

**Giant octopus:** tentacles spread 23 feet (7 meters)

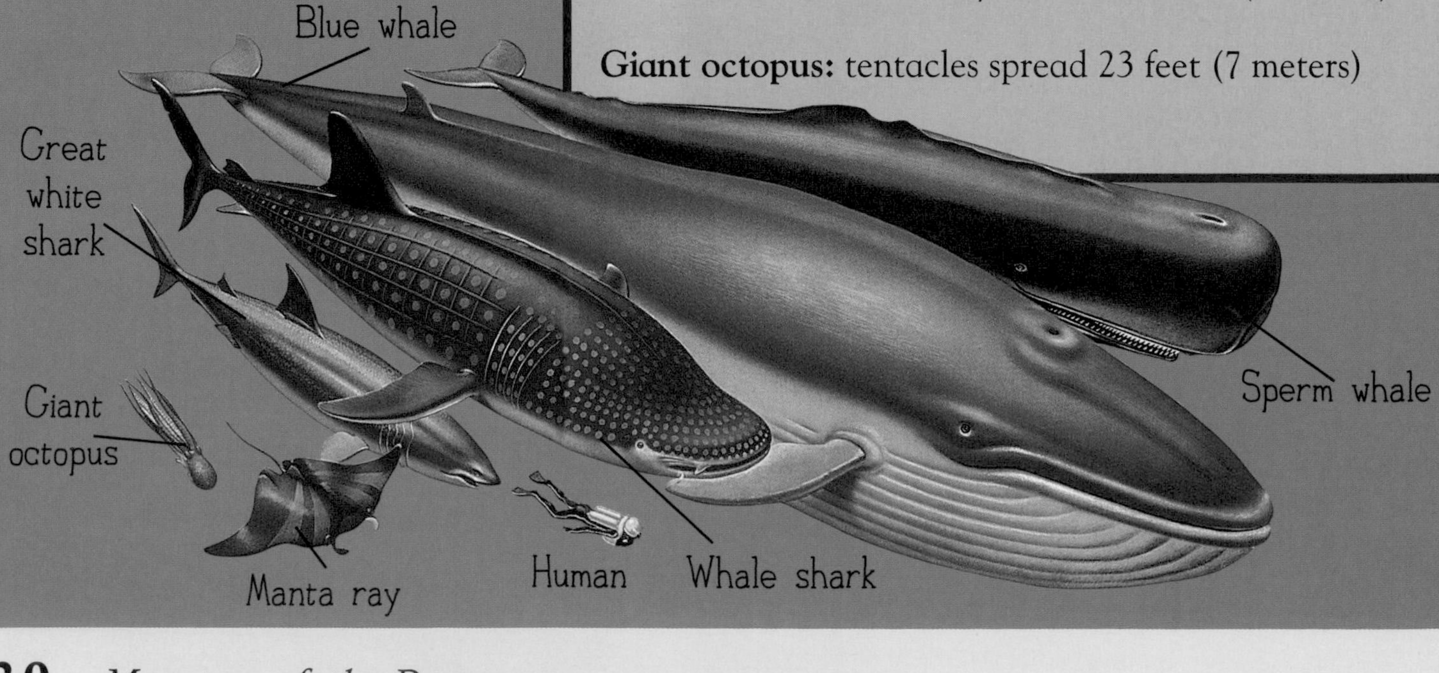

Blue whale

Great white shark

Giant octopus

Sperm whale

Manta ray

Human

Whale shark

# GLOSSARY

**Atoll**
A volcanic island surrounded by a coral reef.

**Baleen**
Describes the comb-like plates of keratin (the same material as fingernails) that hang from the roof of a baleen whale's mouth and allow it to filter food from mouthfuls of water.

**Barbell**
A bristly growth near the mouth of certain fish that detects prey on the seabed.

**Callosity**
A white crusty patch, infested with barnacles, on the head and chin of a Southern Right Whale.

**Camouflage**
The way in which an animal hides from predators, or stalks prey, by blending in with its surroundings.

**Crustacean**
A hard-bodied animal with no backbone, but with many hanging body parts that have a variety of functions, from eating to walking.

**Crustal plates**
Individual sections of the Earth's crust, or skin, which float about on liquid magma. They move against each other to form mountains and other features of the land and seabed.

**Krill**
A shrimp-like crustacean that lives in swarms on the surface of the ocean.

**Magma**
Molten (hot liquid) rock that is formed deep inside the Earth.

**Migration**
The movement of animals to and from particular parts of the ocean, such as feeding and breeding ground.

**Plankton**
Tiny plants (phytoplankton) and animals (zooplankton) that float at the surface of the sea or a lake.

**Plesiosaur**
A long-necked marine reptile that lived during the age of the dinosaurs.

**Polyp**
An animal with no backbone that has a sac-like body with a single opening (its mouth).

**Predator**
An animal that hunts and eats other animals.

**Prey**
An animal that is hunted and eaten by other animals.

**Riptide**
A turbulent area of water where two currents meet.

**Species**
Animals that resemble one another closely and are able to breed together.

**Swim bladder**
The air-filled, balloon-like organ in bony fish that helps them to float.

**Venom**
A poison produced by some animals to repel enemies or catch prey.

# INDEX

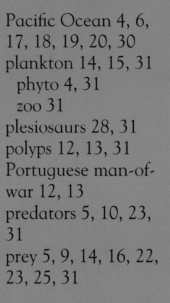